Reaching Back

Reaching Back

Alice Chapin

BETTERWAY BOOKS
Cincinnati, OH

Other fine Betterway Books are available from your local
bookstore or direct from the publisher.

02 01 00 99 98   6 5 4 3 2

Library of Congress Cataloging-in-Publication Data

Chapin, Alice Zillman.
  Reaching back / by Alice M. Chapin.
      p.   cm.
  ISBN 1-55870-454-X (alk. paper)
  1. United States—Genealogy—Handbooks, manuals, etc.
  2. Interviewing. 3. Oral history. I. Title.
CS16.C435   1996
929′.1′072073—dc20   96-32033
                                                 CIP

Interior designed by Jannelle Schoonover
Cover designed by Chad Planner

About the Author

Alice Chapin is the author of thirteen books, including the bestseller *400 Ways to Say "I Love You,"* as well as *A Simple Christmas, 365 Bible Promises for Busy People* and *We're Having a New Baby at Our House*, a children's activity book. Her work has been published in many magazines, including *Guideposts, Family Circle, Woman* and *Moody Monthly*. She lives in Newnan, Georgia.

Contents

Introduction

A few years ago as I was planning a European trip, I discovered that I did not know where my great-grandparents are buried in Germany. I remembered a few things my mother, who is now deceased, had told me about a town west of Berlin that's name began with *S*. But what town? Where was it? Which cemetery? What were my great-grandparents' full names? How I wished that I had written the information down!

There are fascinating facts and wonderful untold stories in every family, but in this busy world many things are left unsaid. We have only a few years to walk through life alongside our parents and grandparents, to learn the uniquely exciting family tales within them. So it is essential that ancestral facts and stories find their place in writing. They form the connecting link between past and future generations that provides an essential sense of belonging for today's often uprooted people.

Did you know that Uncle Dan played the fiddle? Or that Dad drove a tank during the Battle of the Bulge in World War II? Or that Great Aunt Minnie wrote beautiful poetry and that her son Bill ran away forever to Arizona at the age of fifteen? Did you realize cousin Earl and cousin Martha were really first cousins when they married? This type of secret is often locked in people's minds, waiting to be revealed. Most people stop keeping complete family records after the traditional baby book. Precious adult life-facts about beloved forefathers fade quickly or are later distorted as they are chuckled over and passed on by word of mouth. Sometimes a few photographs are preserved, but the figures often seem lifeless, lacking character or feelings. Were those frowning folk really lighthearted children at one time? What made them laugh or cry? What terrible struggles did they endure? Were there persistent health problems you should know about, problems that seem to be passed from generation to generation? There is something inside each of us that cries out for knowledge about the people and events rooted in our past. That's what this book is all about.

You can make an appointment or a series of appointments to spend several hours or a day with Grandma or Grandpa or a cousin, aunt or uncle. Tell the person that you want his or her help to make the spoken history of your family complete. *You* will write down the rich drama for posterity. Some folks are neither inclined nor capable of handwriting journals themselves, but they are usually eager to explore the past with someone who will listen enthusiastically and record it for them. As you talk together, the poignant fears, tears, anger, joys, hopes and dreams of your very own people from yesterday will come alive, primed by questions that gently probe the past, not only for large and small events, but for valuable insights and wisdom.

There will be a bonus. Sharing cherished memories is often profoundly therapeutic for the elderly, giving great satisfaction and enhancing self-esteem as they realize how very valuable they are in helping to track down family chronicles and traditions. And the challenge of filling the last pages with additional recollections, stories, favorite family recipes, and the family tree can provide a wonderful project to occupy long hours after the interviewer leaves.

It is my hope that *Reaching Back*, when completed, will become a priceless heirloom to be treasured and passed on in your family for generations to come.

Alice Chapin
Newnan, Georgia

Tips for Interviewing

Here are a few tips to make your foray into the realm of your family's history a bit easier for both you and the person you are interviewing:

1. Interview your loved one in familiar surroundings that contribute to comfort and ease. Create a relaxed atmosphere with small jokes and casual words to help allay any tenseness that your relative may feel. New events sometimes seem awesome or frightening to a fragile person.

2. Try to follow the questions in order, although you will find conversation often gets ahead of the questions. It helps to be familiar with the questions before you ask them. Nostalgic memories can be extremely emotional. If there are outbursts of tears or anger that result in delay, wait silently or patiently. If there seems to be embarrassment or reluctance to answer a difficult question, pass over it and return to the issue at a later time. But be gentle! Don't push for answers that your relative is not ready to give.

3. You may want to get permission to use a tape recorder or video cassette recorder to capture forever the person's voice or image as you interview. Wouldn't it be wonderful to hear a beloved parent's or grandparent's voice long after they are gone? Be sure to begin each taping session by fully introducing yourselves, giving the names of both interviewer and interviewee and your relationship to each other, and stating the date and place. Explain why you are conducting the interview and that answers to questions are being recorded in the book *Reaching Back*. If a recording is intimidating to your relative, be content with a written record. As you both become more comfortable with the interview process, a short recording may be appropriate.

4. If the person seems to run out of things to say or is not answering fully, wait patiently to give time for deeper thought. Silence is not bad! You can encourage the interviewee to keep talking by assuring her (or him) that you believe she has something vital to say. Tell her that she is an important link in preserving your family's history. Allow your enthusiastic tone of voice and pleasant smile to show how very eager you are to hear about past family events.

   Sometimes it encourages conversation for you to begin a sentence and then stop talking to allow the interviewee to finish. For example, "When your children were naughty and talked back, I guess you . . ." or, "I remember when we went to the dock to greet Uncle Al when he returned from England after World War II. You were there . . ."

   You might use simple prompting statements like, "Tell me what you are thinking about right now." "I guess you must be reliving some of these events over in your mind, right?" or, "Whatever comes to your mind is important; I want to hear it all."

5. Strongly encourage the person to be as explicit as possible about dates (hour, day, month, year), places (include street and number, city,

county, state, name of the country—then and now), complete names (include first, middle and last names, as well as married names and nicknames). In years to come, this information may be all there is to identify long-forgotten family members or locate a homestead or burial place.

6. Some older folks can talk for only short periods of time. Others will be so invigorated by reviewing past memories they will want to go on for hours. Watch for signs of tiring. Several short appointments can be just as fruitful as one long session and may allow your relative time to remember more details between sessions.

Name of interviewer:

Address:

Relationship to person being interviewed:

Place of interview:

Today's date:

Dates of subsequent interviews:

Name of person being interviewed:

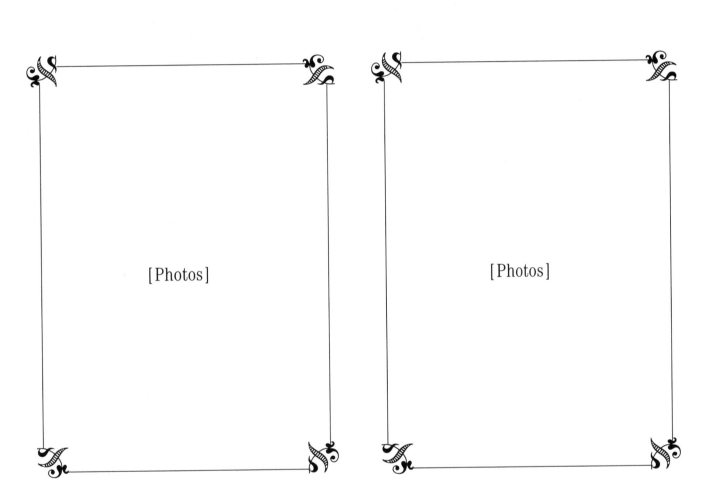

As a child
(When and where was the photo taken?
Who else appears in the photo?)

As an adult
(When and where was the photo taken?
Who else appears in the photo?)

Getting to Know You

What's in a Name?

What is your complete name?

Do you have a nickname?

Where do you live?

How long have you lived here?

With whom do you live?

What is the date of your birth?

Where were you born?

What do you know about the events surrounding your birth?

Why did your parents select your name?

Were you named after someone? Who?

Are you like this person in appearance or personality? How?

What world or national events happened around the time you were born?

Your Family Name

Does your family name have any special meaning? Tell about it.

Where did your family name come from originally? What is its nationality?

Has the spelling of your family name been changed over the years?

What did it used to be?

Why has it changed?

Has the pronunciation changed? How?

Are you related to others whose names are spelled similarly? (Example: Silliman, Zillman, Zillmann)

 Growing Up

Home—The Places You Lived

List, in order, the places you lived while growing up. For each place, be sure to include street and number, city, county, state and name of country. Did your family own or rent? Describe the house. What was the approximate cost of the house or the monthly rent? Why did your family move there? What was the town like? Were you happy there? What events do you remember?

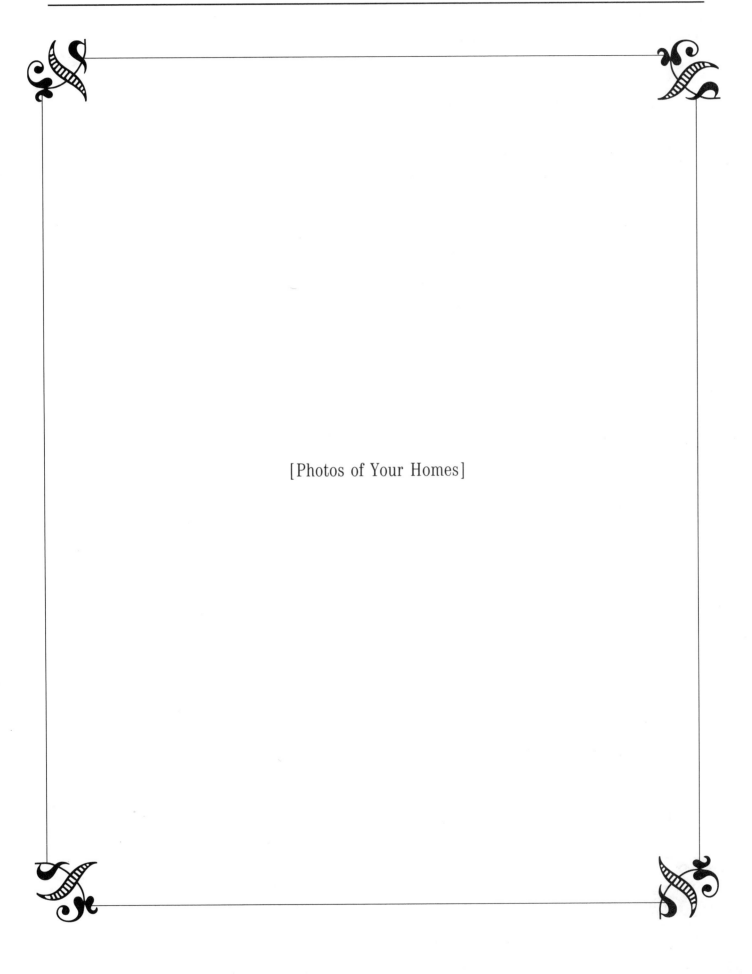

[Photos of Your Homes]

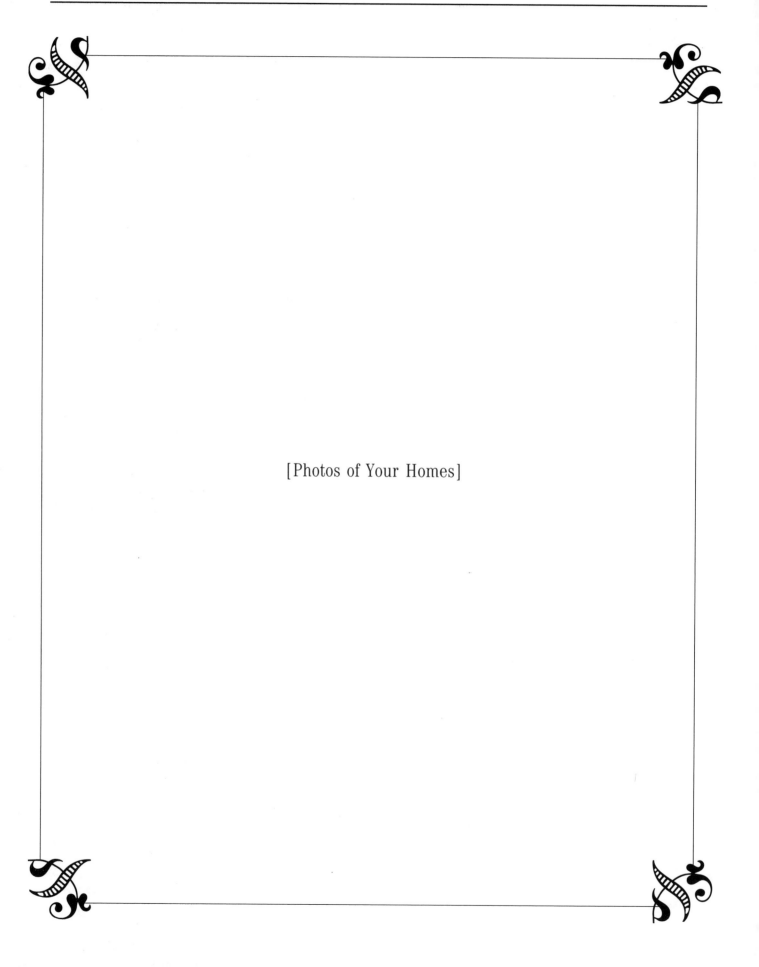

[Photos of Your Homes]

Your Childhood

What do you think you were like as a child?

What did others say about you?

Can you remember interesting or humorous stories that other folks shared about your very early childhood?

What is the earliest thing you can remember? Why do you think you recall this so clearly?

What kinds of things did you particularly like to do as a child?

Did you like to play alone? What did you play?

Who was your favorite playmate?

Can you remember a favorite toy? Describe it. Where did it come from?

Did you have a favorite private place to play as a child?

What were some of your secret thoughts as a child?

How did you spend your happiest hours?

Did you like to read? Who taught you? What were some of your favorite books and authors?

Did you play a musical instrument? Who taught you? How good were you?

Did you have a favorite relative? Who was it?

    Why was this person a favorite?

    What kinds of things did you do together?

    Describe the person.

What person did you admire most outside your own family? Why?

Were you healthy as a child?

What childhood diseases did you have? At what age?

What chronic illnesses did you experience? What were the symptoms? What treatment did you receive? Was the treatment difficult? Did you spend time in the hospital? How did your illness affect the rest of the family?

Do you remember any important family illnesses? What were they? Which members of your family had them?

Do you remember your first experience with death? Whose death was it? Did you attend the funeral? How did it affect you? What did the person mean in your life?

What was the most traumatic event in your early childhood?

What was the happiest event in your early childhood?

Which important world and national events were taking place during your early childhood years?

Your Teen Years

As a young person what were your favorite

foods?

sports?

games?

seasons?

movies or movie stars?

music and music groups?

hobbies?

kinds of clothing?

places to go?

What goal did you have in life as a young person? Why? Did you reach that goal?

What special dislikes or fears did you have growing up? Why?

What made you happy as a young person? Why?

What made you sad? Why?

Describe how you looked in your teen years. Tell weight, height, hairstyle, clothing, etc.

Describe your teen years. Were they wonderful? Traumatic? Lonely? Troubled? Sad? Why? Recall some incidents.

Did you smoke or drink during your teen years?

What one person had the greatest influence on your life as a young person? Why was this person special to you? What was the person like?

Did you have a special friend your own age as a young person? Who was it?

Where did that person live?

What kinds of things did you do together?

Can you remember a story of something you did together?

What was the most traumatic event in your teen years?

What was the happiest event in your teen years?

Do you remember your first job? What was it?

How old were you?

What company or person did you work for?

How did you get the job?

Did you like the job? Why?

Were you a hard worker?

How much were you paid?

How did you spend the money?

Which important world and national events were taking place during your teen years?

Your Hometown

Of all the places you lived, which do you consider your hometown? Why?

How old were you when you lived there?

What important world and national events took place during the years you lived in your hometown?

Describe your hometown in those days.

Was it a big city? A suburb? A rural town? What was the population?

Were there sidewalks?

Was there a library? Describe it.

Was there a movie theater?

What were people like in your hometown area?

Did you enjoy living there?

What do you remember about downtown or where your family shopped?

How often did your family go shopping? Did you go along?

What were favorite stores or other places?

What was unique about your hometown?

Did the part of town where your family lived have a special name?

Describe the area.

What was the street name and number of your family's house?

Describe the outside of your house, including type of construction, design, color, yard, garden, trees.

Describe the inside of your house.

What was the furniture like?

How many rooms were there?

What was your room like? Did you share with someone?

What kind of heating system? Furnace? Wood or coal stove?

Were you warm?

How did you get water? Hot water?

Describe the kitchen, including stove, refrigerator or ice box, counter space and appliances.

How many bathrooms were there? Inside or outside?

Did the house have electricity? Do you remember when it was installed?

Who were favorite neighbors? What did they mean to your family?

Have you visited your hometown lately? How has it changed—for better or for worse?

School Days

Did you attend preschool or nursery school? If so, where?

Where did you attend elementary school?

How many years did you complete?

What kind of student were you?

Did you have a favorite subject? A least favorite subject?

Can you remember some teachers? Tell about a few.

Describe some memorable incidents. What happened?

What were the classrooms like?

Describe the bathrooms.

Where did drinking water come from?

How did you get to school? How far was it from your home?

Did you bring lunch? Where did you eat?

What kinds of clothing did you wear to school?

What were hairstyles like?

What fads do you remember?

How were kids disciplined in school? Were you ever disciplined in school? Tell about it.

Who were your best school friends? Where did they live? Do you remember some things you did together?

Can you remember stories of things that happened in your hometown school?

Did you attend high school?

How many years did you complete? What year did you graduate?

What kind of student were you?

Did you have a favorite subject? A least favorite subject?

Can you remember some teachers? Tell about a few.

Describe some memorable incidents. What happened?

Were you happy in high school? Why or why not?

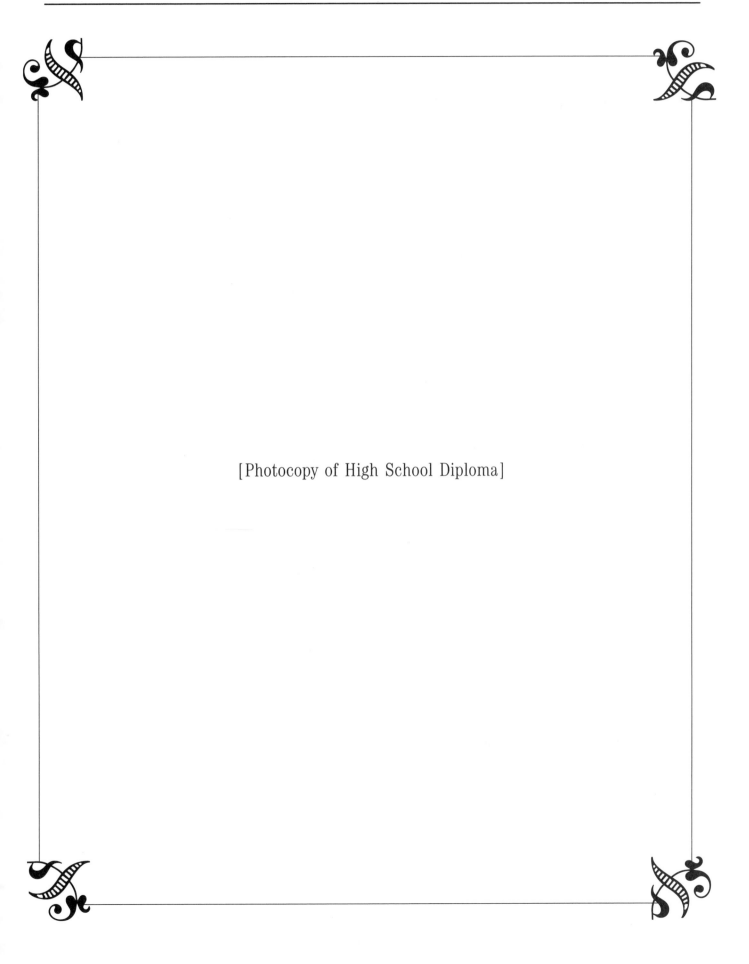

[Photocopy of High School Diploma]

Did you attend college? Where?

How many years did you complete? Did you graduate? When?

What kind of student were you?

What was your major? Your minor?

Where did you live while attending?

Describe your college years.

Can you remember interesting or humorous incidents?

Were you happy in college? Why or why not?

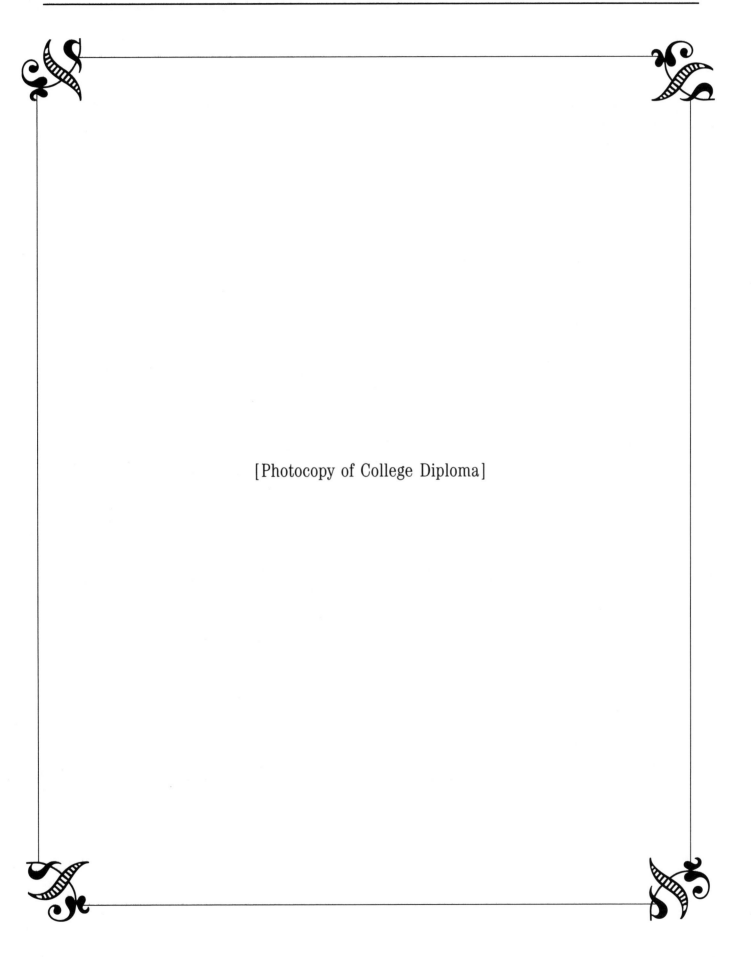

[Photocopy of College Diploma]

Family Life

Describe your family members. Were they hard-working? Close? Intellectual? Musical? Involved in politics? Other?

How is your family outstanding or different?

What language did your parents speak at home? Did they teach you? Why?

Were there grandparents, aunts, uncles or other relatives living in your parents' home? Who? Why were they living there? How did you feel about having them there? What did they mean to you?

What things did your family like to do together?

Do you remember any special trips or vacations your family took?

Recall a few times when you or others were disciplined.

What unusual family sayings or expressions do you remember? What did they mean? Where did they come from? Are these expressions still used in the family today? When?

What values were important to your parents?

Did your parents smoke? Drink? Dance?

What did your parents want you to become? Why?

Were there favorite home remedies for sickness? What were they? Did they work?

What skills did your parents teach you?

What household jobs were you expected to do? Did you have an outside job?

Did you have any pets? Describe them?

Where did you get them?

Who took care of them?

Did your family own a radio or television? What were favorite programs? What did they mean to your family?

Was your family religious?

Did you attend a house of worship and religious classes together? How often?

Which house of worship did you attend? Where was it? What denomination?

Do you remember the spiritual leader's name?

What activities did you and your family get involved in?

Did your family have devotions and prayer at home? Describe these.

How did your family survive difficult times? Do you remember a few?

How did you celebrate holidays? What customs, ceremonies, decorations or foods do you remember at these celebration times?

What family traditions can you remember?

How was a death observed? Was there a wake? A long period of mourning?

What were your mother's favorite dishes to cook? Were those your favorite ones to eat? (Be sure to write recipes in the back of this book.)

What kind of music was popular when you were growing up? Did your parents like your favorite music groups and songs?

What possessions did you and your family particularly value? Why?

Do you remember any family secrets you can share?

 Love and Marriage

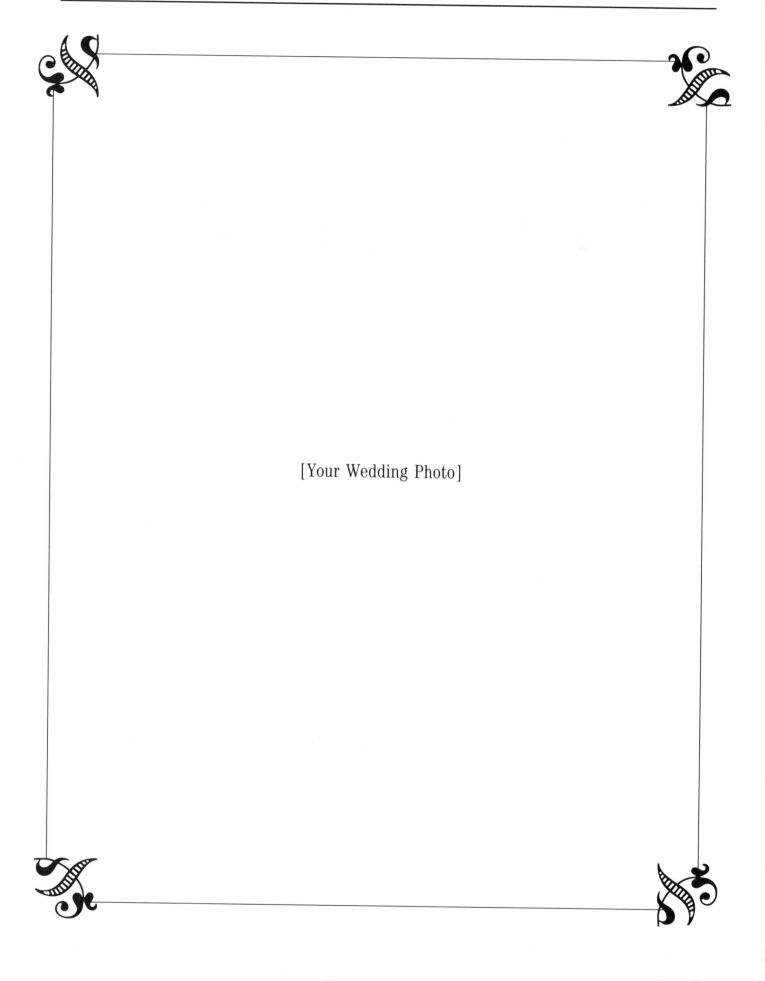

[Your Wedding Photo]

Your Courtship

How did you and your spouse meet?

How old were each of you?

Did you like each other right away? Why?

What did you do on your first date?

What was dating like then?

What kinds of things did you like to do together?

How long was your courtship?

Your Wedding

What was the date of your wedding?

Where was your wedding held? Describe the place.

Who officiated?

What did you wear at the wedding? Describe clothing, hats and shoes.

Who were your attendants? What did they wear?

Describe the wedding ceremony.

Did you have a reception? Describe it. Where was it held?

Where did you go on your honeymoon?

What world or national events were taking place at the time you were married?

[Copy of Wedding Certificate]

[Newspaper Clippings About the Wedding]

Your First Home

Where was your first home located? Give street name and number, city, county, state, name of country.

Why did you choose this place?

Did you rent or own? What was the monthly payment? What was the value of the house?

How old was the house?

Describe the outside of the house.

Describe the inside of the house.

What was your favorite room in that house?

Describe the kitchen and bathrooms.

Do you remember your neighbors? Who were they? Why were they important to you?

Did both of you work? What job did each of you have? Where did you work? What was your income?

What did it cost for a week's groceries? For a loaf of bread? A dozen eggs? A pound of hamburger?

What were the most difficult adjustments in your early years of marriage? Why?

Was marriage what you expected? Why?

Did the two of you argue? About what? How did you settle arguments?

Recall one or two best parts of your early marriage.

What would you change about your early years together?

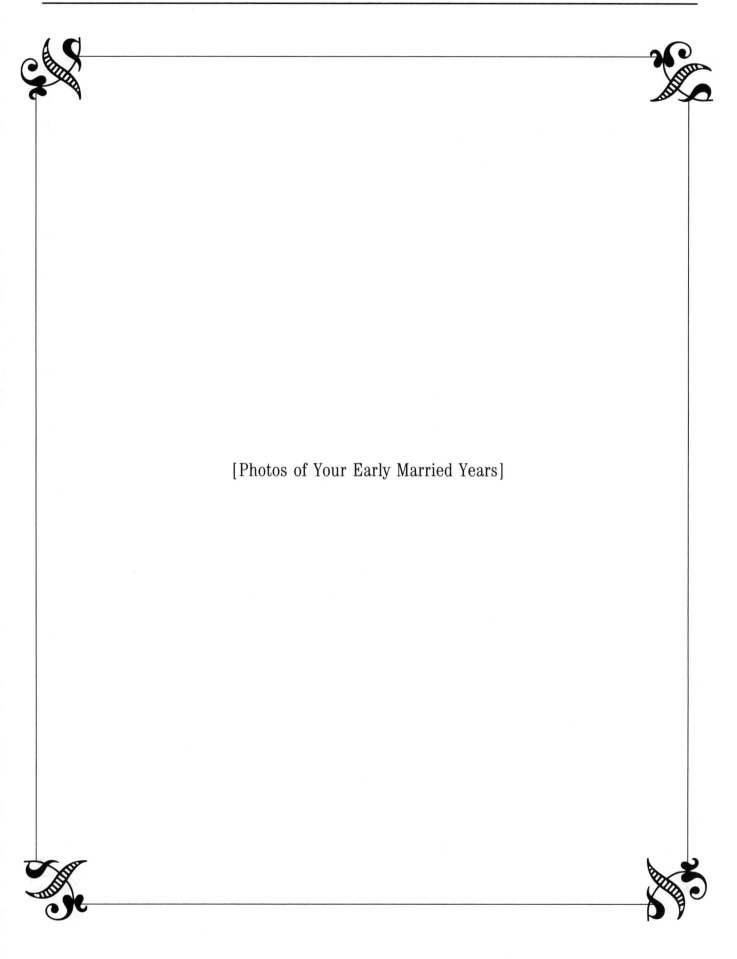

[Photos of Your Early Married Years]

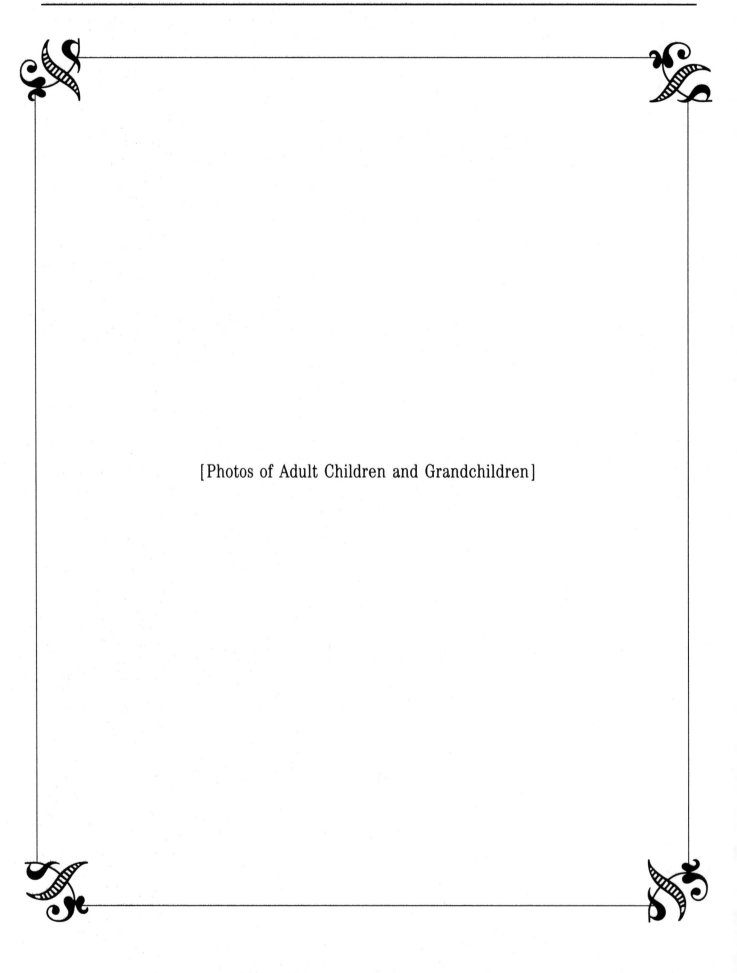

[Photos of Adult Children and Grandchildren]

[Photos of Adult Children and Grandchildren]

Later Married Years

List the homes you lived in. Tell approximate dates and why you moved. Recall important events that took place in each.

What is the best place you ever lived? Why?

Recall some of the happiest events of your later married years.

What were the sad moments in your marriage?

What were some of the funniest incidents of your later married years?

What is the most significant thing you learned from being married to your spouse?

How long were you married? How did your marriage end?

Were there other marriages? To whom? How old were you?

How long were you married? How did the marriage end?

 Children

(or Nephews and Nieces)

Your Young Children

How old were you when your first child was born?

Where was your first baby born?

Who helped you in delivery?

Was your first an unusual birth?

Was it difficult or easy to have a child then?

List your children in order of birth. Include full names and nicknames, birthdates and places.

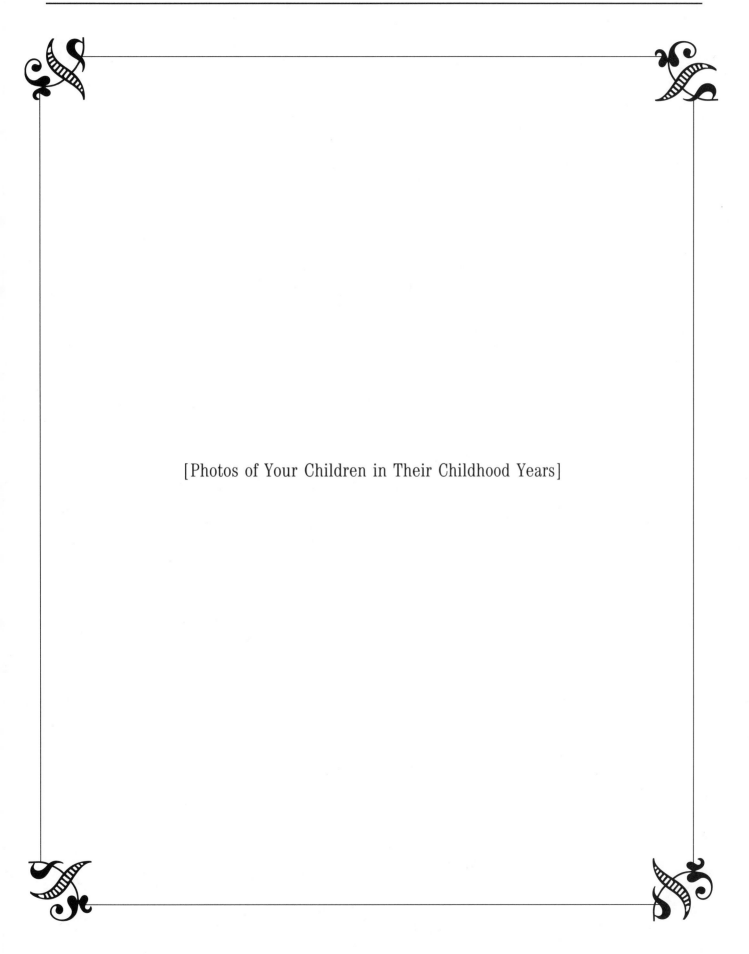

[Photos of Your Children in Their Childhood Years]

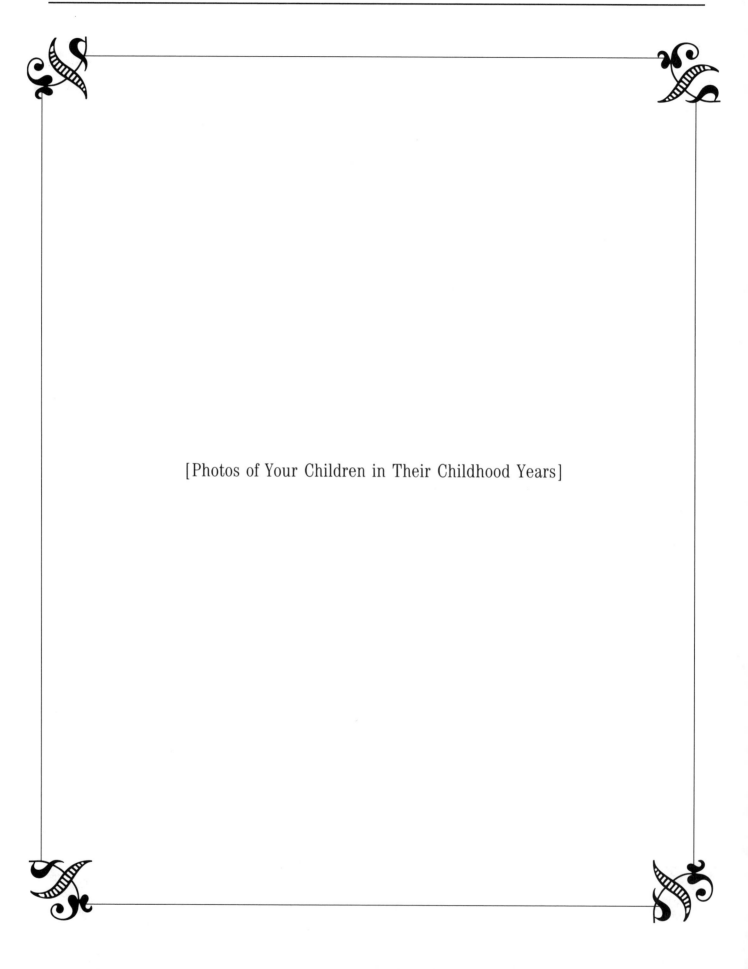

[Photos of Your Children in Their Childhood Years]

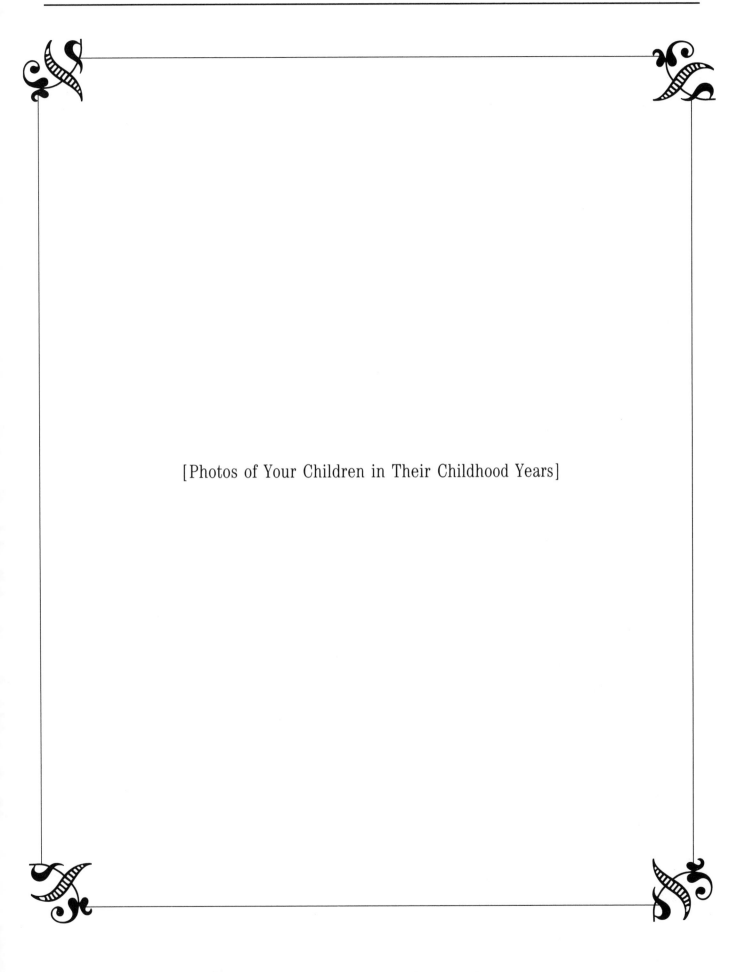

[Photos of Your Children in Their Childhood Years]

Did any of your children die? What were their names? How did they die, and how old were they? How did the deaths affect you?

If there were stepchildren, foster children or adopted children, give their names and nicknames. Tell about each and why they were with your family.

Did you have favorite child-rearing theories?

What was it like to be a parent then?

What kind of disciplinary methods did you use?

Do you recall special difficulties in rearing your children? Talk about a few times that were unusually hard for you. What happened?

Did some of your children give more trouble than others? Why?

What values did you most want to teach your children? Did you succeed?

Adult Children

Where are your children now?

If they are married, what are the names of their spouses?

Grandchildren

List the names and ages of your children's children.

What do you most enjoy about your grandchildren (or nephews and nieces)?

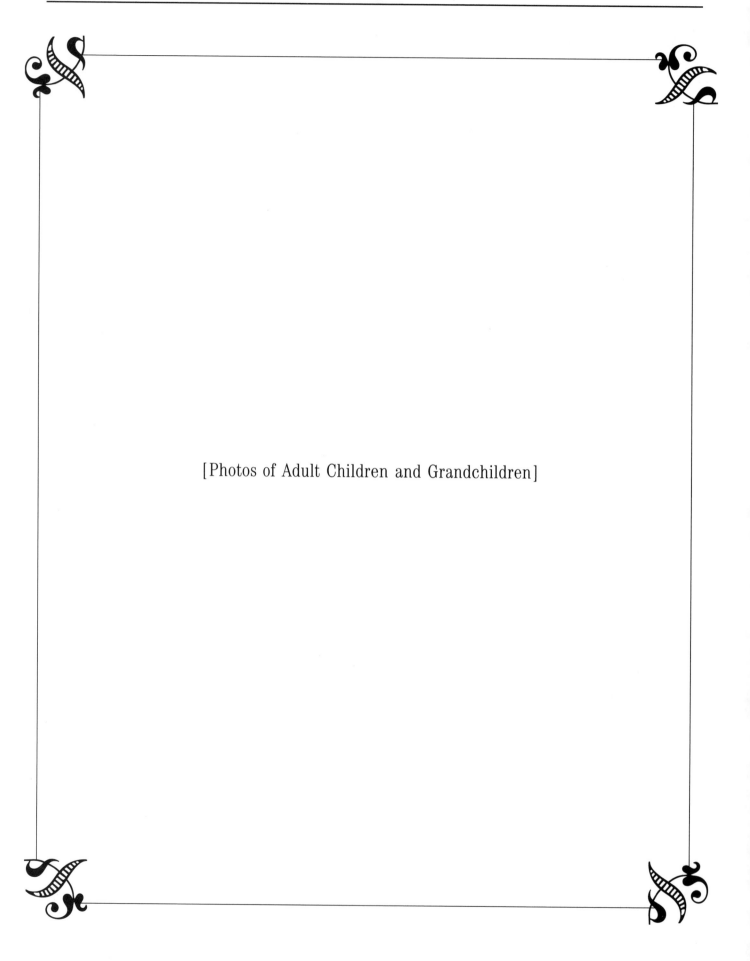

[Photos of Adult Children and Grandchildren]

[Photos of Adult Children and Grandchildren]

[Photos of Adult Children and Grandchildren]

About Your Life

Work

What jobs have you held in your lifetime? List them in order. Tell where and when you worked, the nature of the job, hours, salary, and whether or not you enjoyed the job. Recall your boss and co-workers.

How did you prepare for your major profession?

Did you specialize?

Why did you choose this line of work?

What did you like most about it? Why?

What did you like least about it? Why?

How many years were you in your major profession?

Did the nature of your work change over the years? How?

Did you change major professions? Tell about your second line of work.

What was your avocation, something you did apart from work?

Were you ever in the military? For which country? Which branch? What was your rank? How long did you serve? Were you drafted or did you volunteer? Did you make it a career? What was your job? Where were you stationed? Were you involved in any wars or specific battles? Which ones? Were you wounded? Can you tell any stories about this part of your life? Did you receive any medals or awards or decorations? Why?

What jobs did your spouse hold during your married years? List them in order. Tell where and when your spouse worked, the nature of the job, hours, salary and whether or not the job was enjoyable.

How did your spouse prepare for a major profession?

Did your spouse have a second line of work?

Spiritual Journey

Do you consider yourself a religious person today?

What are your basic religious beliefs?

Where did you get these beliefs?

What is the most important part of your faith?

Has your idea of important religious beliefs changed over the years? How?

In past years, were you more or less religious than you are now? Explain.

Is religious community important in your life now? Which religion or denomination?

Has a religious community always been important to you?

What have been your favorite religious activities over the years?

Which religious communities have you belonged to in your adult years? Include the names of houses of worship, denominations, locations, names of spiritual leaders, numbers of years attended and when attended. Tell why you chose each community or denomination and why you left.

Were you baptized? At what age? When? Where? By whom? If you were baptized as an adult, what made you decide to take this step?

[Copy of Baptismal Certificate]

Was there one particular event that highlighted your spiritual experience? What happened? When? How did you change?

What person(s) most influenced your spiritual life? Why?

What is your view of God?

Has prayer been an important part of your life over the years?

How often do you pray? When? How?

Is reading scripture important to you? Has it always been?

Have you memorized portions?

What are some of your favorite passages?

Do you have a favorite religious song? What is it? Why?

When you need to be uplifted in spirit, what do you do?

What private inspirational thoughts can you share?

Which spiritual beliefs do you most want for your children, grandchildren, or nieces and nephews?

Why do you believe you were put here on earth?

Goals and Achievements

Have you attained your major goals in life?

What accomplishments are you most pleased with?

Do you have any secret or unfulfilled ambition(s)?

What dreams or goals do you have today?

Personal Growth

What personal qualities in your life have improved most over the years? How?

Describe your attitude, outlook and philosophy today.

How have you changed over your lifetime?

Sharing Your Wisdom

What major principle for living would you like to pass on to your grandchildren or nieces and nephews? Why?

What advice would you give young people today?

What advice would you give newlyweds?

What spiritual words of wisdom would you like to give your children and grandchildren (or nieces and nephews)?

Ups and Downs

What has been the happiest part of your life?

What has been the unhappiest part of your life?

What has been the hardest struggle? Did you overcome it? How?

What has been the most disappointing part of your life?

What was your biggest mistake? What has been your biggest lesson learned?

If you could live your life over, how would you change it?

Were there certain turning points in your life? Describe them. How did things change? How did you change?

History in Your Life

What was the most terrible world or national event you can remember in your lifetime? How did it affect you?

What was the most wonderful world or national event you can remember in your lifetime? How did it affect you?

What can you remember about other well-known events? World War I, World War II? The sinking of the Titanic? The Great Depression? Presidents? Your first radio? Walking on the moon? New inventions? Other memorable world or national events?

[Newspaper Clippings of Major Events]

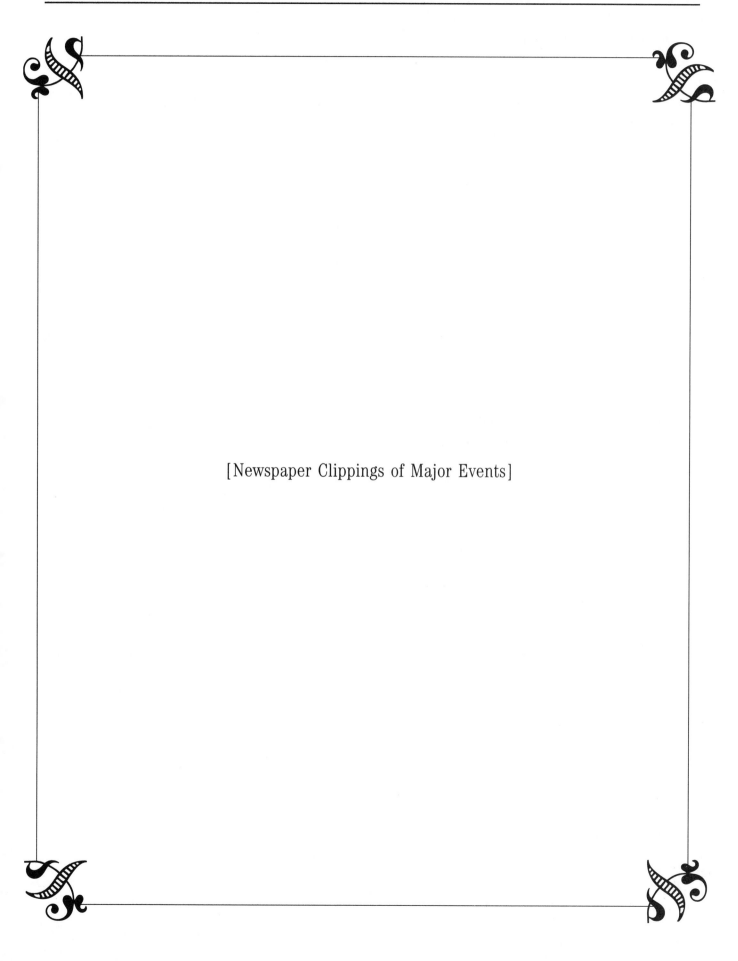

[Newspaper Clippings of Major Events]

Important People

Is there one person whom you have turned to for help over and over? Who is it? Talk about these times. How were you helped?

Tell about special friends, including character traits, skills, occupations, places they lived and where they are today. Tell a story about each.

[Photos of Your Special Friends]

Recall an unusual friend or relative. Why was this person important in your life?

Talk about another person who affected your life—a sweetheart, a family boarder, a significant relative. Tell about character traits, skills, occupations, etc. Why was this person important in your life? Can you remember a story about this person?

Today

What person do you most admire today? Why?

How many languages do you speak? How did you learn them?

How do you presently spend your most enjoyable hours? Why?

What kinds of things do you like to do?

Which person helps you most today?

# Parents

Your Mother

What was your mother's full maiden name?

Did she have a nickname?

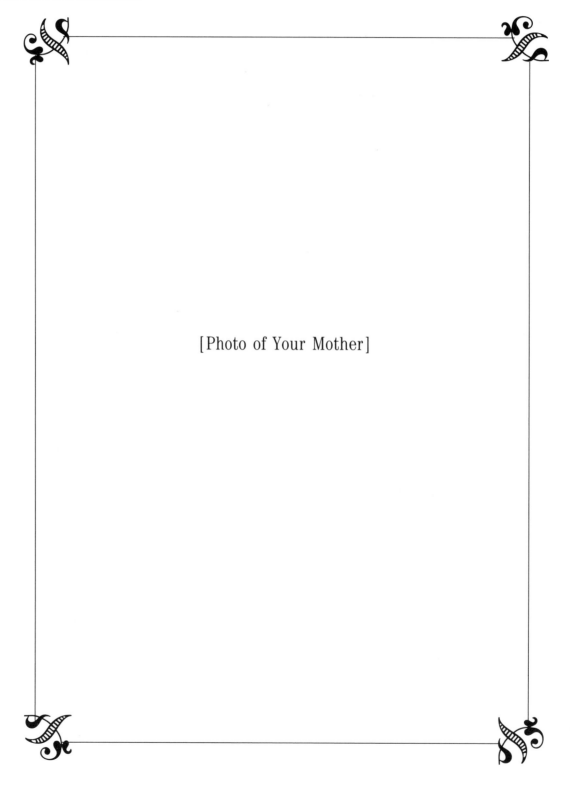

[Photo of Your Mother]

Where was your mother born?

What is the date of her birth?

Do you know anything about the birth?

How many years of school did she complete?

Where did she attend

elementary school?

high school?

college?

Describe your mother. What was the color of her eyes? Of her hair? Was she tall or short, heavy or light? What was her most outstanding physical characteristic?

What was your mother like? Was she happy-go-lucky? Outgoing? Shy? Humorous? Intellectual? Career-minded? Other?

What special talents or skills did your mother have? Music? Art? Drama? Dancing? Writing? Storytelling? Hospitality? Other?

What hobbies did she have?

What did she particularly like?

What did she particularly dislike?

Did she have favorite sayings?

Did your mother work outside the home? What was her occupation?

> What were her places of employment?

> What do you think her income was?

Was your mother in good health? If not, talk about her illnesses.

> What were her symptoms?

> What was the treatment?

> How did her health affect you?

What do you think your mother was like as a young girl?

Was your mother a religious person?

What religious community was she brought up in? What denomination was it?

What house of worship did she attend when you lived at home? Where is it located? What denomination is it?

Was she involved in religious activities? Which ones?

What was her private spiritual life like?

Did she change spiritually over the years? How? What caused the change?

What people were important in her spiritual life?

When and how did your mother die?

Where was she living at the time of her death?

What were your feelings about your mother's death?

Where is your mother buried? Why was this place chosen?

Your Father

What was your father's full name?

Did he have a nickname?

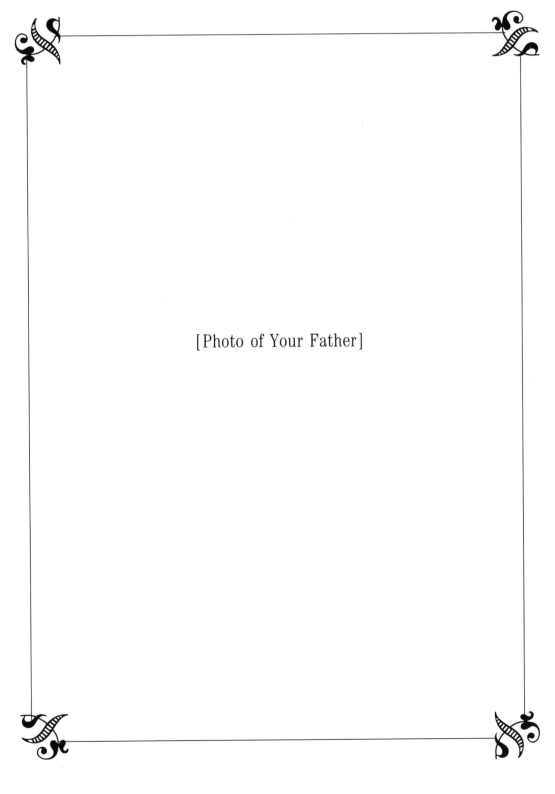

[Photo of Your Father]

Where was your father born?

What is the date of his birth?

Do you know anything about the birth?

How many years of school did he complete?

Where did he attend

    elementary school?

    high school?

    college?

Describe your father. What was the color of his eyes? Of his hair? Was he tall or short, heavy or light? What was his most outstanding physical characteristic?

What was your father like? Was he happy-go-lucky? Outgoing? Shy? Humorous? Intellectual? Career-minded? Other?

What special talents or skills did your father have? Music? Art? Drama? Dancing? Writing? Storytelling? Hospitality? Other?

What hobbies did he have?

What did he particularly like?

What did he particularly dislike?

Did he have favorite sayings?

What was your father's occupation?

What were his places of employment?

What do you think his income was?

Was your father in good health? If not, talk about his illnesses.

What were his symptoms?

What was the treatment?

How did his health affect you?

Was your father in the military? For which country? Which branch? Was he drafted or did he volunteer? What was his job? What was his rank? How long did he serve? Where was he stationed? Was he involved in any wars or specific battles? Have you heard stories about these? Was he ever wounded? Did he receive medals or decorations? What were they? Why did he receive these awards?

What do you think your father was like as a young man?

Was your father a religious person?

What religious community was he brought up in? What denomination was it?

What house of worship did he attend when you lived at home? Where is it located? What denomination is it?

Was he involved in religious activities? Which ones?

What was his private spiritual life like?

Did he change spiritually over the years? How? What caused the change?

What people were important in his spiritual life?

When and how did your father die?

Where was he living at the time of his death?

What were your feelings about your father's death?

Where is your father buried? Why was this place chosen?

Life Together: Your Parents

How did your parents meet?

When and where were your parents married?

Do you know any details of the wedding?

Who were the attendants?

Who officiated?

Did your parents have a honeymoon? Where did they go?

Did your parents move from another country? Which country? Why?

Where did they live in the old country?

Do the old country and their old town have the same names today?

What part of the homeland is their town located in? Do you know the names of nearby towns? (Locate them on a map.)

What was life like in the old country?

How did your parents make a living in the old country?

Did you talk to your parents about their move? Was the trip difficult? Why? How did they travel? Where did the money come from? Who came with them? What possessions did they bring? In what city did they arrive?

Where did your parents settle in their new land?

What was their first home like? Where was it?

How did they make a living once they arrived?

What do you think their life was like?

Did your parents speak English? Which language did they speak?

What kinds of things did your parents like to do together?

In what ways were your parents unusual or outstanding?

What was their biggest struggle? How did they handle it?

What was their greatest joy?

How did they discipline the children? Which parent was the strongest in the area of discipline? Give examples.

What did you like most about your parents?

What did you like least about them?

Did you favor one parent over the other? Why?

List the children in your family in order of birth. Include full names and nicknames, birthdates and places, and names of spouses. Tell about each.

Did any children die? What were their names? How did they die, and how old were they? How did the deaths affect you?

If there were stepchildren, foster children or adopted children living in your parents' home, give their names and nicknames. Tell what you can about each and about why they were living with your family.

Grandparents

Your Maternal Grandmother

What was your maternal grandmother's full maiden name?

Did she have a nickname?

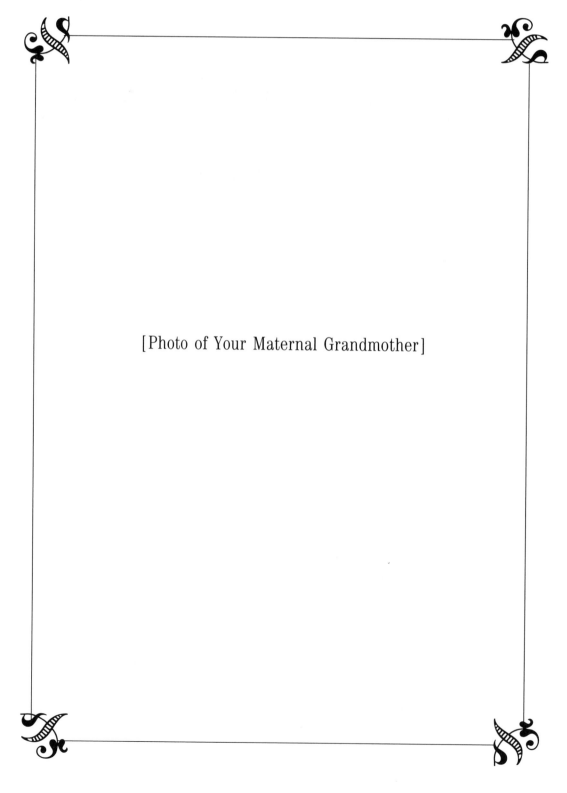

[Photo of Your Maternal Grandmother]

Where was your maternal grandmother born?

What is her birth date?

What do you remember best about her?

What do you know about your grandmother's parents?

What was your grandmother like? Was she happy-go-lucky? Outgoing? Religous? Shy? Humorous? Intellectual? Career-minded? Other?

Do you recall your grandmother's special talents, skills or hobbies?

How many years of school did she complete? Where?

What was her occupation?

Describe your grandmother. What was the color of her eyes? Of her hair? Was she tall or short, heavy or light? What was her most outstanding characteristic?

Was your grandmother in good health? If not, describe her illness, symptoms and treatment.

When and how did your grandmother die? What do you remember about her death?

How did it affect you?

Where is your grandmother buried?

Why do you think this place of burial was chosen?

Your Maternal Grandfather

What was your maternal grandfather's full name?

Did he have a nickname?

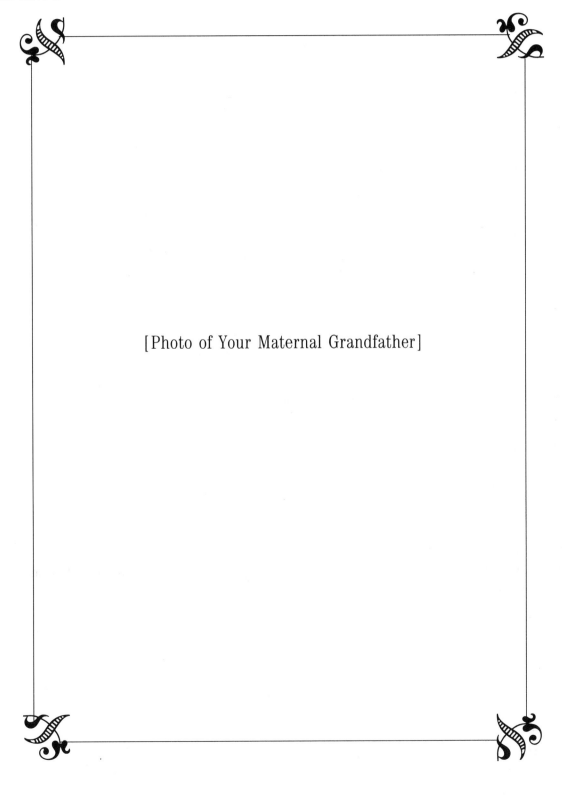

[Photo of Your Maternal Grandfather]

Where was your maternal grandfather born?

What is his birth date?

What do you remember best about him?

What do you know about your grandfather's parents?

What was your grandfather like? Was he happy-go-lucky? Outgoing? Religous? Shy? Humorous? Intellectual? Career-minded? Other?

Do you recall your grandfather's special talents, skills or hobbies?

How many years of school did he complete? Where?

What was his occupation?

Describe your grandfather. What was the color of his eyes? Of his hair? Was he tall or short, heavy or light? What was his most outstanding characteristic?

Was your grandfather in good health? If not, describe his illness, symptoms and treatment.

Was your grandfather in the military? For which country? Which branch? Was he drafted or did he volunteer? What was his job? What was his rank? How long did he serve? Where was he stationed? Was he involved in any wars or specific battles? Have you heard stories about these? Was he ever wounded? Did he receive medals or decorations? What were they? Why did he receive these awards?

When and how did your grandfather die? What do you remember about his death?

How did it affect you?

Where is your grandfather buried?

Why do you think this place of burial was chosen?

Life Together: Your Maternal Grandparents

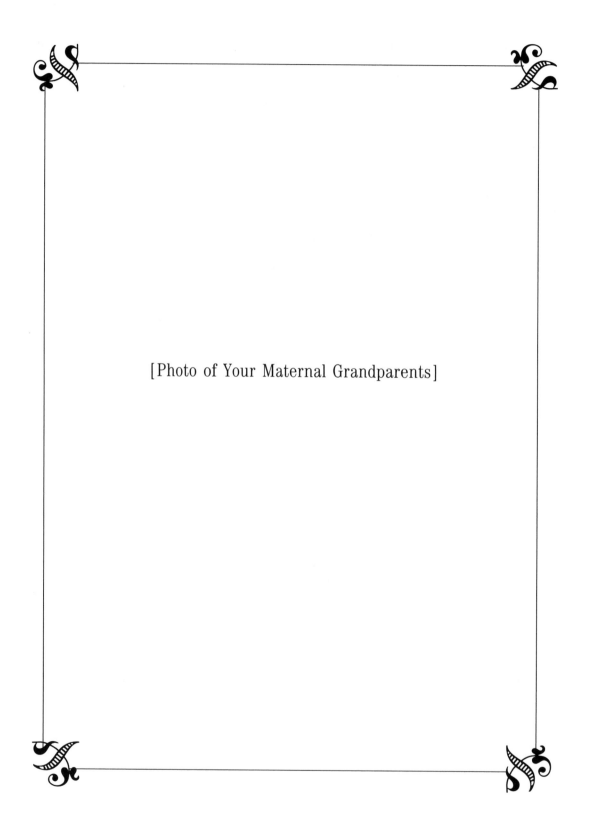

[Photo of Your Maternal Grandparents]

When and where were your maternal grandparents married?

Recount any details of the wedding you have heard about.

How did they meet?

Do you recall any interesting stories about them?

Did your maternal grandparents move from another country? Which country was it, and why did they leave?

Where did they live in the old country?

Do this country and their old hometown have the same names today?

What part of the homeland is their town located in? Do you know the names of nearby towns? (Locate them on a map.)

Did they tell you what life was like in the old country? Share their memories.

How did your grandparents make a living in the old country?

Did you talk to your grandparents about their move? Was the trip difficult? Why? How did they travel? Where did the money come from? Who came with them? What possessions did they bring? In what city did they arrive?

Where did your grandparents settle in their new land?

What was their first home like? Where was it?

How did they make a living once they arrived?

What do you think their life was like?

Did your maternal grandparents speak English? Which language did they speak?

List the children of your maternal grandparents (your aunts and uncles) in order of birth. Include full names and nicknames, birthdates and places, and names of spouses. Tell what you can about each.

Did any of your grandparents' children die? What were their names? How did they die and how old were they?

If there were stepchildren, foster children or adopted children living in your grandparents' home, give their names and nicknames. Tell what you can about each and about why they were living with your grandparents.

Your Paternal Grandmother

What was your paternal grandmother's full maiden name?

Did she have a nickname?

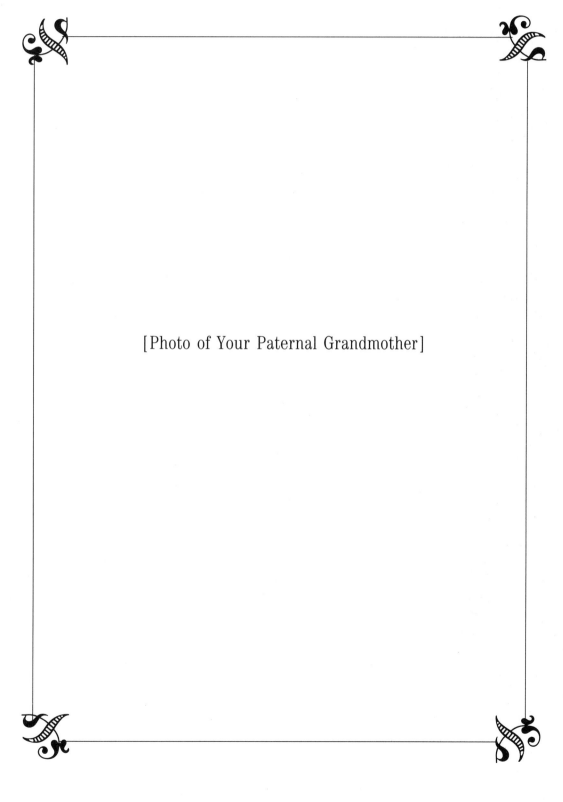

[Photo of Your Paternal Grandmother]

Where was your paternal grandmother born?

What is her birth date?

What do you remember best about her?

What do you know about your grandmother's parents?

What was your grandmother like? Was she happy-go-lucky? Outgoing? Religous? Shy? Humorous? Intellectual? Career-minded? Other?

Do you recall your grandmother's special talents, skills or hobbies?

How many years of school did she complete? Where?

What was her occupation?

Describe your grandmother. What was the color of her eyes? Of her hair? Was she tall or short, heavy or light? What was her most outstanding characteristic?

Was your grandmother in good health? If not, describe her illness, symptoms and treatment.

When and how did your grandmother die? What do you remember about her death?

How did it affect you?

Where is your grandmother buried?

Why do you think this place of burial was chosen?

Your Paternal Grandfather

What was your paternal grandfather's full name?

Did he have a nickname?

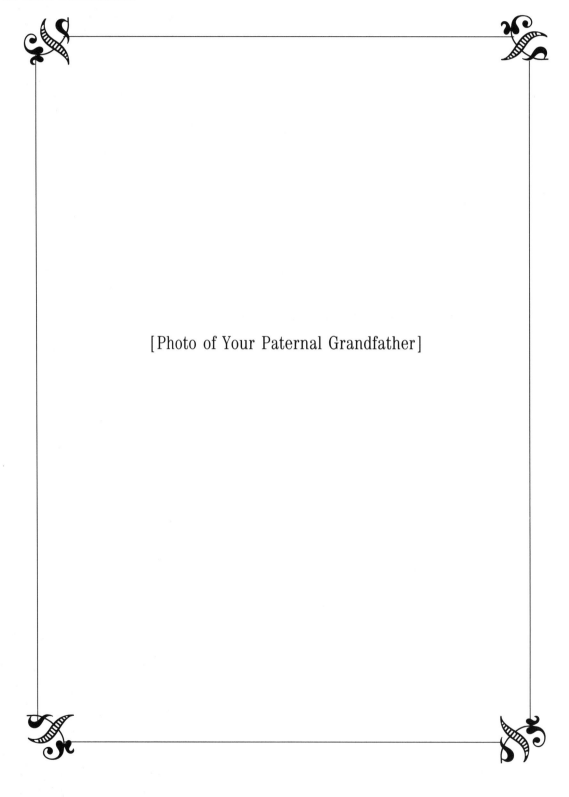

[Photo of Your Paternal Grandfather]

Where was your paternal grandfather born?

What is his birth date?

What do you remember best about him?

What do you know about your grandfather's parents?

What was your grandfather like? Was he happy-go-lucky? Outgoing? Religous? Shy? Humorous? Intellectual? Career-minded? Other?

Do you recall your grandfather's special talents, skills or hobbies?

How many years of school did he complete? Where?

What was his occupation?

Describe your grandfather. What was the color of his eyes? Of his hair? Was he tall or short, heavy or light? What was his most outstanding characteristic?

Was your grandfather in good health? If not, describe his illness, symptoms and treatment.

Was your grandfather in the military? For which country? Which branch? Was he drafted or did he volunteer? What was his job? What was his rank? How long did he serve? Where was he stationed? Was he involved in any wars or specific battles? Have you heard stories about these? Was he ever wounded? Did he receive medals or decorations? What were they? Why did he receive these awards?

When and how did your grandfather die? What do you remember about his death?

How did it affect you?

Where is your grandfather buried?

Why do you think this place of burial was chosen?

Life Together: Your Paternal Grandparents

[Photo of Your Paternal Grandparents]

When and where were your paternal grandparents married?

Recount any details of the wedding you have heard about.

How did they meet?

Do you recall any interesting stories about them?

Did your paternal grandparents move from another country? Which country was it, and why did they leave?

Where did they live in the old country?

Do this country and their old hometown have the same names today?

What part of the homeland is their town located in? Do you know the names of nearby towns? (Locate them on a map.)

Did they tell you what life was like in the old country? Share their memories.

How did your grandparents make a living in the old country?

Did you talk to your grandparents about their move? Was the trip difficult? Why? How did they travel? Where did the money come from? Who came with them? What possessions did they bring? In what city did they arrive?

Where did your grandparents settle in their new land?

What was their first home like? Where was it?

How did they make a living once they arrived?

What do you think their life was like?

Did your paternal grandparents speak English? Which language did they speak?

List the children of your paternal grandparents (your aunts and uncles) in order of birth. Include full names and nicknames, birthdates and places, and names of spouses. Tell what you can about each.

Did any of your grandparents' children die? What were their names? How did they die and how old were they?

If there were stepchildren, foster children or adopted children living in your grandparents' home, give their names and nicknames. Tell what you can about each and about why they were living with your grandparents.

More About the Family

Tracking Down the Family

Does your family have one or two "black sheep" relatives? Who were or are they? Why are they "black sheep"? Where are they today?

Are there any little known relatives living in distant places here or abroad? Give names, relationships to you, approximate age, names of their parents and side of the family, and complete address if available. Do you remember these people? Can you remember any stories about them?

Do you know the whereabouts of important or interesting family documents like wills, scrapbooks, school diplomas, war uniforms and medals, wedding or birth certificates, letters, passports, handcrafted items, photographs, silverware, dishes, jewelry, or other items that should be preserved and passed on? Who owns them? Where are the items stored? Tell what you can about each.

Will you help label old photographs and other family documents so that relatives will be able to identify them? (Be sure to attach identifying sticker including full name of each person in photographs.) Write down names of original owners of various other items and tell whatever you can about the history of each piece.

Can you suggest other people to interview who might be knowledgeable about past family events? Give the name, relationship, address. Why do you suggest these folks? Tell what you remember about each.

Your Mother's Family Tree

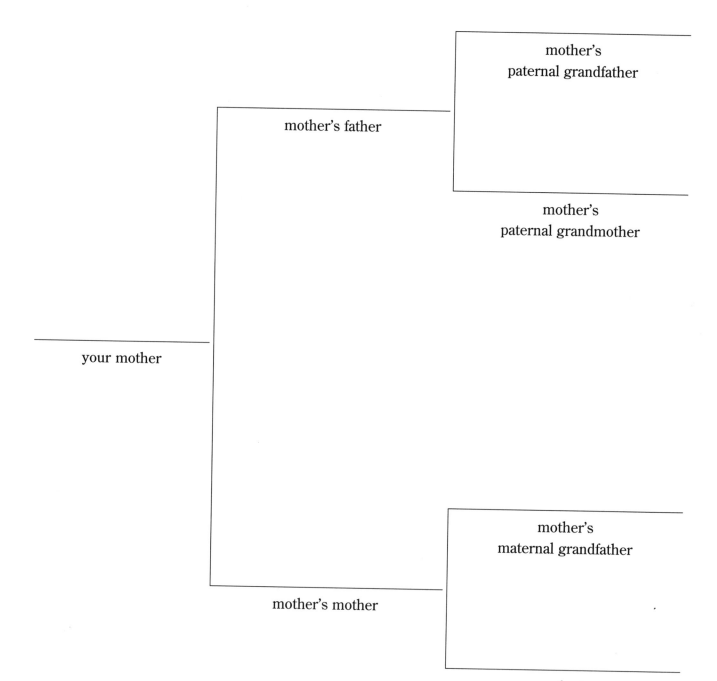

mother's
paternal grandfather

mother's father

mother's
paternal grandmother

your mother

mother's
maternal grandfather

mother's mother

mother's
maternal grandmother

Your Father's Family Tree

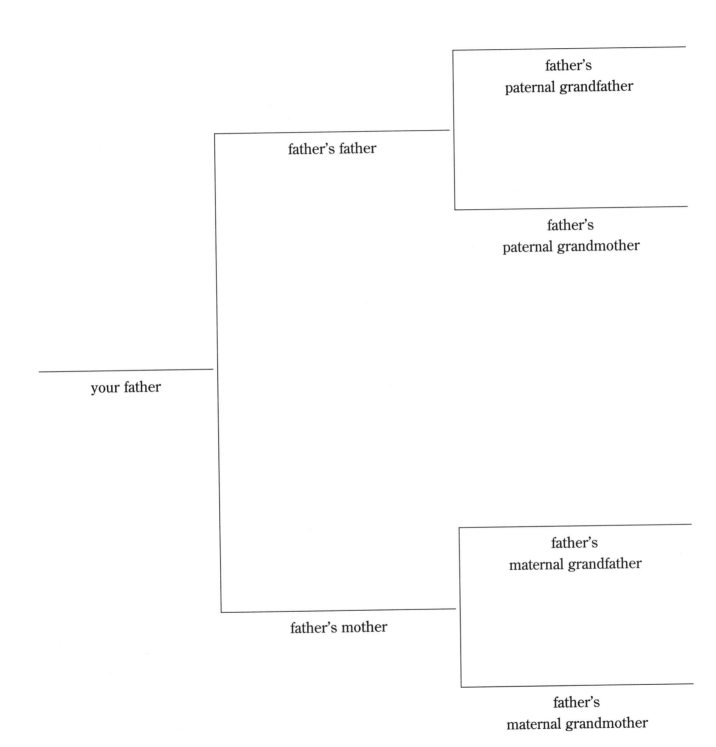

father's
paternal grandfather

father's father

father's
paternal grandmother

your father

father's
maternal grandfather

father's mother

father's
maternal grandmother

Favorite Family Recipes

Be sure to list the source of the recipe, and when and how these foods were served.

Birth and Marriage Records

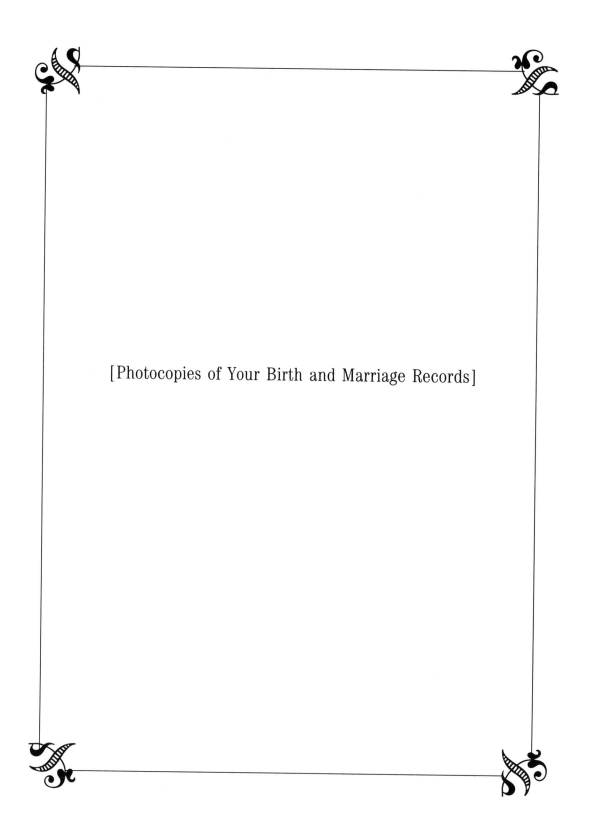

[Photocopies of Your Birth and Marriage Records]

[Photocopies of Your Birth and Marriage Records]

[Photocopies of Your Birth and Marriage Records]

[Photocopies of Your Birth and Marriage Records]

Other Family Photos

[Photos of Your Family]

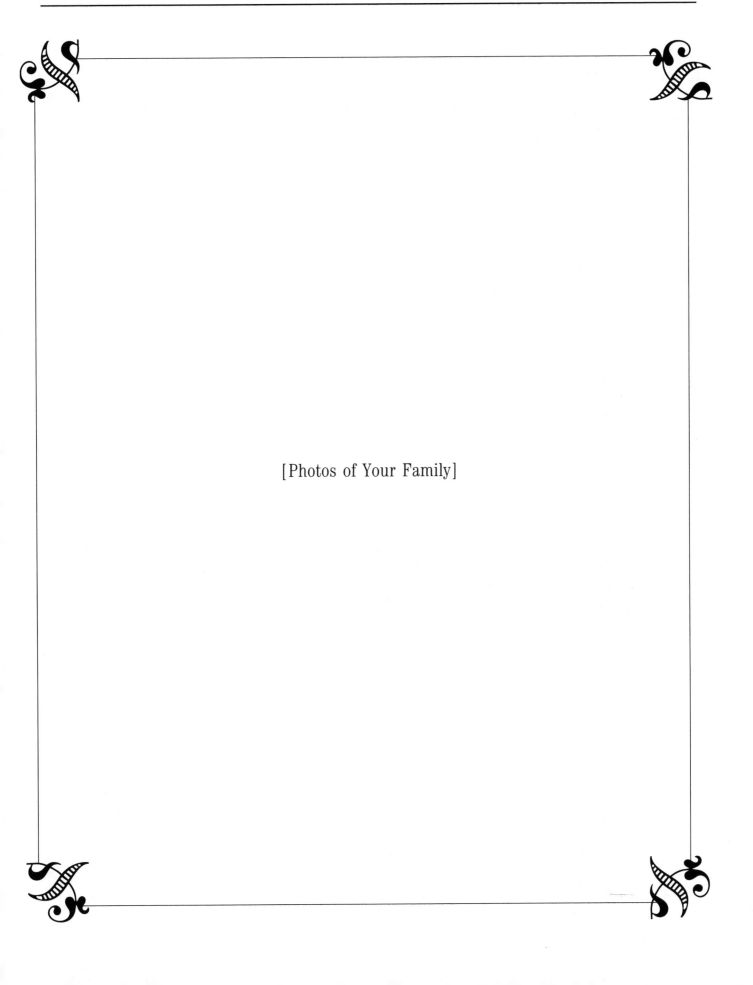

[Photos of Your Family]

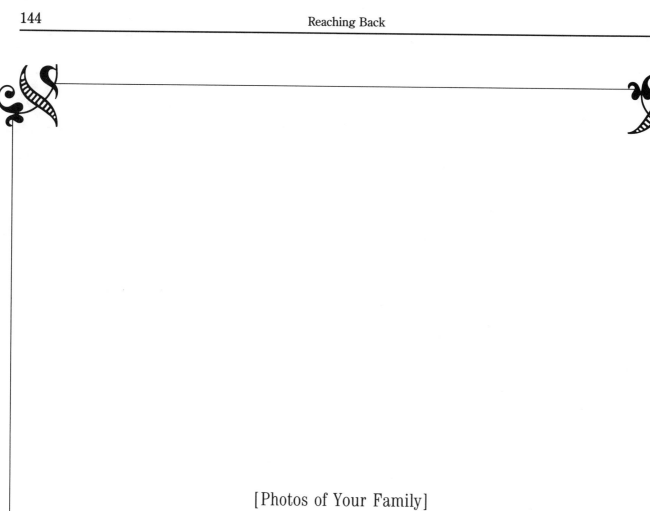

[Photos of Your Family]

[Photos of Your Family]

[Photos of Your Family]

[Photos of Your Family]

Your Favorite Family Stories

More Great Books Full of Great Ideas!

The Unpuzzling Your Past Workbook: Essential Forms and Letters for All Genealogists—Now unpuzzling your past is easier than ever using 42 genealogical forms designed to make organizing, searching, record-keeping and presenting information effortless. *#70327/$15.99/320 pages/paperback*

Unpuzzling Your Past: A Basic Guide to Genealogy, 3rd ed.—Make uncovering your roots easy with this complete genealogical research guide. You'll find everything you need—handy forms, sample letters and worksheets, census extraction forms, a comprehensive resource section, bibliographies and case studies. Plus, updated information on researching courthouse records, federal government resources and computers on genealogy. *#70301/$14.99/180 pages/paperback*

Writing Family Histories and Memoirs—From conducting solid research to writing a compelling book, this guide will help you recreate your past. Polking will help you determine what type of book to write, why you are writing the book and what its scope should be. Plus, you'll find writing samples, memory triggers and more! *#70295/$14.99/272 pages/paperback*

How to Write the Story of Your Life—Leave a record of your life for generations to come! This book makes memoir writing an enjoyable undertaking—even if you have little or no writing experience. Spiced with plenty of encouragement to keep you moving your story toward completion. *#10132/$13.99/230 pages/paperback*

Turning Life Into Fiction—Learn how to turn your life, those of friends and family members, and newspaper accounts into fictional novels and short stories. Through insightful commentary and hands-on exercises, you'll hone the essential skills of creating fiction from journal entries, identifying the memories ripest for development, ethically fictionalizing other people's stories, gaining distance from personal experience and much more. *#48029/$14.99/208 pages/paperback*

Writing Life Stories—Author Bill Roorbach shows you how to turn life events into vivid personal essays and riveting memoirs. Learn how to open up memory, access emotion and shape scenes from experience, as life events become fascinating plot lines. *#48035/$17.99/224 pages*

Charting Your Family History: The Legacy Family Tree Software Solution—Combine the power of CD-ROM with the hands-on guidance of a sourcebook! Capabilities include unlimited data input for multiple generations of ancestry, picture and sound links, and over 20 different reports, including pedigree charts, timelines and more. *#70420/$49.95/270 pages/150 b&w illustrations/paperback + CD-ROM*

The Handybook for Genealogists, 9th ed.—This comprehensive research aid will save you hours of work with each listing. Includes state-by-state directories of archives and libraries, county listings, custody information, state profiles, color maps, migration routes and more—all completely updated. *#70411/$34.99/380 pages/ 60 color maps*

First Steps in Genealogy—Packed with friendly advice and practical information, this superb guidebook helps you define your goals and uncover facts about people behind the names and dates. Included are sample forms, a glossary of genealogical terms and an archive directory. *#70400/$14.99/128 pages/paperback*

The Internet for Genealogists, 4th ed.—Using basic language and easy, step-by-step guidance, this book places a wealth of information at your fingertips, no matter what your computer skill level. Included is an overview of basic computer hardware and software, Web browsers and E-mail, addresses for more than 200 genealogy megasites, libraries and catalogs, as well as a detailed glossary of over 160 computer terms. *#70415/ $16.99/192 pages/paperback*

Family Reunion Handbook, 2nd ed.—From record keeping to planning menus, this guidebook provides you with hundreds of resources, tips and ideas for organizing family reunions in all sizes, themes and locations. A special scrapbook section offers great ideas for showcasing family pictures and letters, and preserving them for future generations. *#70416/$14.99/288 pages/100 b&w illustrations/paperback*

Fun & Games for Family Gatherings—In this indispensable guide, you will find more than 235 games, ideas and activities for creating cherished memories shared by family members of all ages. *#70417/$12.99/ 144 pages/50 b&w illustrations/paperback*